The Beginning of My BS

Roma Mazumdar

ARCHWAY
PUBLISHING

Archway Publishing books may be ordered
through booksellers or by contacting:

Archway Publishing
1663 Liberty Drive
Bloomington, IN 47403
www.archwaypublishing.com
1 (888) 242-5904

ISBN: 978-1-4808-8277-5 (sc)
ISBN: 978-1-4808-8276-8 (e)

Library of Congress Control Number: 2019914556

Print information available on the last page.

Archway Publishing rev. date: 10/10/2019

Acknowledgements

This book would have not been possible without the help of Stephanie Spaete, Malloy Phillips, and Archway Publishing.
Thank you Miss Spaete for appreciating my poetry and encouraging me in a way which made me comfortable and confident.
Thank you Mrs. Phillips for giving me so much of your time to solely help me edit.
Thank you to my sister for answering my late night calls, forever indebted to you.
Thank you Rylee Ferguson for being an amazing artist.
Chloe Barker, always my astronaut.
Thank you Peyton Williams for breaking my walls.

Pieces

Preface

I read a poem once
It made me feel things
It made tears grow from my eyes
It made me see differently.
I'd like to create something that did the same one day.

My First Ever

It's thrown and tossed as if it were a ball that didn't matter
    if lost
So casually as if it was dust; flowing and growing out of
    our mouths
With ease we spit it out.
For some receiving it, it's like a bullet striking you in the
    back
But for some others it is just another added to the stack.
It has lost its meaning for we have used it too much
But still onto this word we strongly clutch
We so heavily fiend to hear it we hardly care if they mean it
In the moment it makes us feel needed and wanted
But soon this memory will feel haunted.
But then it comes down to this;
What does it mean?
Or what did it mean
This thing we all think we've seen in movies and books
I mean they are always the best hooks.
This thing with varied definitions
This thing that everyone around me pretends to know
But never really show
This "it", this "thing", I speak of is something I don't
    understand
This it, this thing, is love

Piece 1

Pessimism, the Harder Parts, I am Not a Nihilist, I Swear...

Naïve Dreams

I'm not satisfied.
Satisfaction is for fools
Happiness is for fools
Love is for fools.
I want to be one of those fools
I want to breathe their air
I want to feel their ignorance.
Their bliss.

Cold Car

The whole car ride was so depressing
It was raining harder than you could imagine
Still, when I think back on it, I can hear the heavy pattering,
It was a loud ride
But not loud with voices
It was loud with everything but voices.
The rain smashing onto the windshield, the music, and other cars speeding by
I thought all these sounds would fill the uncomforting silence
But they did nothing except shine a spotlight on the lack of speaking.
I wanted to say something
I really did
But my ego was bigger than me
And I guess so was hers so we just sat there in silence for what felt like forever.
There was intensity in our silence as if it were competitive
You could feel the anger in the car
I didn't need to see her face and she didn't need to say anything, her body just let off an angry wave that was streaming right at me

Sad Wealth

It really does seem like money could buy happiness, huh?
I mean look at all the celebrities
They have it all, right?
Except peace
Except sanity
They go in and out of rehabs like it's their second home.
My family has money
We live in a big house
My friends tell me they dream of living here.
But the thing is, my family is the unhappiest bunch you could meet
My dad is angry and my mom is sad
Money couldn't make us happy
The material joy only lingers for a breath
And then disappears for a lifetime.

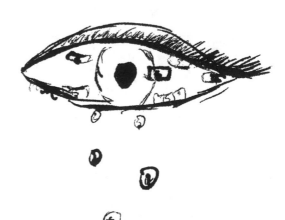

Undeserving

I can see her pain
I want to ease it.
It's in her eyes
Her voice
Her every movement
It's stitched into her skin.
I want to rip it out
I'll swallow it myself.

It Won't Exist

I am unable to make a sound when I cry
Just heavy breaths.
If I cannot hear it, it's not happening.
I don't look in the
mirror when I cry
If I can't see it, it's
not happening.
I don't want to be
weak.
So, I lie to myself
instead.

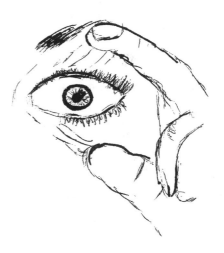

Mistake

I wondered if I hadn't said anything what would've happened
If I had just kept my mouth closed
If I had just had more self-control
Things could be different.
Better.

Stupid Holiday

Why do people create hopeless resolutions only on New
    Year's?
Any moment in time is a moment you can change
Every second is a second you can recreate yourself.
So why do we wait around for this certain over-hyped night
    that occurs every 12 months to think that anything is
    possible?
If it is possible on this one night it is possible every day.

Elastic

We live with nets in our stomach.
When they feel empty, we fill them with material
But the nets never actually get filled
They just sag lower and lower.
These nets are elastic
Adding materials doesn't fill our voids
It just makes them heavier
And soon these nets will consume us.

FIRE

The fire always dies
no matter how
hard we try to
keep it alive
We can try to feed
it with sex and
therapy but no
flame is eternal.

Desert

How do I make this
river stop flowing?
It's starting to hurt
I would think my eyes
would be dry by now.
But they keep going
And I don't know why
Or how to stop it.

You wouldn't be invited anyway

This must be my funeral.
I'm laying here with no sense of life left
My body feels numb
And my eyes are swollen shut.
I dug my own grave
And now no one's here to say goodbye
I'll write my own obituary
And sign my death certificate
with my blood.

Bore

I get bored easily.
So I create problems
I create drama.
That's a lie
I realize now I do it because I am afraid people will get
bored of me.

My Idea

It hurt when they told me the truth
I wasn't angry
I wasn't frustrated
Just hurt.
This whole idea I had was stripped from my heart with the
    maneuver of a tongue.

Bad Casting

The best actors I know aren't on TV
They're in my home
My school
All around me.
They can fake happiness
Love
Sadness
And anger the best I've ever seen.
These actors around me should really be cast in roles
They're the ones who belong on the big screen
Because all they do is act.
It's honestly impressive
You should see how my family can flip their emotions like
 a light switch
They'll shriek with anger, but when you walk in, the switch
 will flip and they'll be the happiest you've seen.
Honestly, I'm impressed

PARENTAL ADVISORY: NON-RELIGIOUS LYRICS

So many great people taken away far too early
Too many lost faces
Lost lives
Lost joy
for what.
I think if there's a man up there he's not doing too well
Too many of the bad guys are getting away
And too many good ones are being taken.

I don't think we are chess pieces on a board being placed in
    certain spots by a man upstairs
Or that there's a "plan" for all of us

Or a purpose.
I think that idea
makes it seem
like nothing we
do or say has
any value
We are not
where we are
because of a
plan
We are where
we are because
of our actions
You aren't successful because a god wanted you to be

You're successful because you worked your ass off.
If there is a man up there, I want to know what his plan was
    for every good life that was lost so brutally
The ones who were burned
The ones who drowned
The ones who were shot
What was their purpose??

Pessimist Subconscious

I must be going crazy.
I hear whispers being poured in my ear
Like lava they flow in softly but then they burn into my head.
It's not me
I think it is my subconscious
My subconscious must be a nihilist
Because the words she uses are brutal.

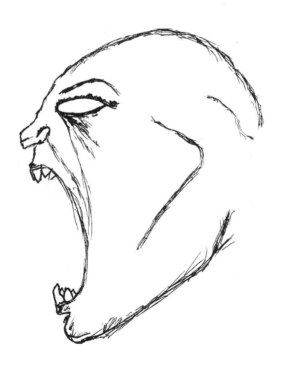

Tear Machine

He pulled tears out of her eyes
As if she was his dispensary.
With the swift movement of a finger she would fall to his command.
Attention was the only currency she needed.

Cold Blood

The seasons must have sped up
It wasn't her time
Yet I still watched her shed tears as if they were her second
skin.

Gamer

I must stop being a fool and losing the games that I create in my own head.

POSITIVE

Tomorrow is a new day, right?

Then why do they all feel the same?

Every new day is the same just progressively worse.

I try to look forward to things

But as I get older the abundance of those things seems to
     be shrinking

Wind Blowing

You thought if I burned, you'd finally feel my warmth
But there is no warmth there
Just a cold breeze.

I Shouldn't Say This

I want this plane to crash
I want to fall in the water and drown a bit but then survive.
But I don't understand why
I think a lot of us feel this way sometimes.

False Reality

Being on the brink of death makes us feel the most alive.
I bungee jump
And I feel alive
I sky dive
I feel alive
I sit alone at the dinner table
And feel dead inside.
It doesn't make sense.
Why would being so near to death make me feel full of life
While real life makes me feel diseased

Seconds

There are those moments where I feel happy.

Alive.

I forget about all the sorrow

All of reality

But then I leave and I'm alone with my mind and it all

begins to hurt again.

Drano

He tried flushing himself down the toilet
He wouldn't fit
He didn't belong there
With one hand he held the knob and with the other tried
shoving his body down

Winter

It's cold out here
But I have a coat for my body
Gloves for my hands
Some socks for my feet.
But how do I warm my heart?

Piece 2

Growing Pains

Plants

We're all overwatered, trying our best to grow and sprout on our own, but that's not enough. They want more, we should grow faster, sprout higher and bloom bigger. They do everything in their power to speed up our process, they feed us fertilizers of all sorts, fertilizers we don't need, fertilizers we aren't ready for.
They don't realize that all we need are the simple things: sun, water, and love.

They try to pull out our weeds.
They don't realize our weeds are what we truly are and once they are gone, we are no longer us, we are the plant they want to see.
We look better from the outside without our weeds, I guess.

They overwater us, thinking we will grow faster, no.
We drown, we can't handle it, we try to breathe, we try to
    swim, we do, but that's not how it works
That's how you kill a plant.
Haven't you heard?
If you overwater a plant, it'll die.

Same Cycles

We all enter this world in the same way, just in different
    places
Put in different religions
Different levels of wealth
Different love
Different environments and surrounded by different people
We're told different purposes.

We all leave this word in the same way
Our hearts can no longer function as we want.
Just in different places
Different after lives according to the religion we were
    placed in
Different levels of wealth
Different love
Different environments
Surrounded by different people
Just for different reasons.

Our cycles are the same
So why do we differentiate, why do we create all these
    barriers between ourselves?

So what causes all the hate
What causes all the neglect?
The thing is, there's no one to blame because it's not we who
    decide where or when we enter this world.

Our thoughts are different because of the people we come
    from, theirs are different because of the people they
    came from and so on.
But that's not true either
Because we can change our minds
We can change our religion
We can change our environments
We can change the people we're surrounded by
We can change our wealth.

Yeah it's hard as hell but possible.

Fake Stranger

I have changed a lot
The idea of being surrounded by people used to fuel me
But now I push away
I've been pushing everyone out of my life.
And why?
That's the thing I can't figure out
Walking through the halls used to be a blast, filled with
    interaction and hugs
Now I shove past everyone and pretend to be a stranger.
I used to be bold, outgoing, always looking to party
But that title has changed.
I surround myself with only a small group
I realize now that those things do not bring me joy anymore
I don't even know if it ever did
I'm looking for something more.

Who is she?

I looked at her
We made eye contact.
I was disgusted
She had changed so much
She was a corrupt person now
She was screwed up
I wanted to punch her.
But if I did this, my knuckles would be bludgeoned bloody
with glass
The girl I was looking at was myself
I was looking in the mirror
I was 15.
15 was when I saw how much I had changed and I was
disgusted.

Happy New Year!

Another new year
But nothing's new.
I caught myself not even noticing the time when the clock
    hit 12 this year
I was too preoccupied.
But then I remembered how this moment used to fill me
    with hope and excitement
And the farther down my memory I go, the more I remember
    how much I used to care for this "moment".

I think the older we get, the less and less hopeful New Year's gets
It just becomes an excuse to get messed up and show off.
I think it's because with age we get more realistic and we realize that this moment is just like any moment (only with more alcohol) and a cooler name
Or maybe I have just lost all hope.

Don't Give Her Sad Eyes

Where the sun sets is where I want to be
It seems good there
Alone
And peaceful.
She never loses.
But then the sun rose and whispered something to me
She said she's the winner everyday
She outshines everybody
She hates it.
She's alone
She said winning isn't fun when you have no one to celebrate
with.
I used to always watch her with envy
But now I look at her with sad eyes.

Mask

A façade is an outward appearance that is maintained to
conceal a less pleasant or credible reality
I think I am a little farther off from less pleasant
And this façade is getting harder and harder to keep up.
People are starting to notice
I can feel my mask slipping
And I can feel people drifting away.
I am not the bad ass who doesn't give two shits
The mask is starting not to fit
I think I am getting too big for it
I wish I could glue it to my face and keep it on forever
I wish I could go to the store and buy a new one.
But it's too late
They've already seen me without it
They've seen me care.

Deteriorate

I watched her destroy herself
With white lines up her nose
And red ones up her wrist.
They were more than an outcry for attention.
Her cuts weren't thin
These lines were thicker and deeper.
She grew up too fast.
Two parents
But not a single role model
One was an absent alcoholic
And the other did not know how to raise a child.
She thought she knew it all
She learned to hate herself at a young age
Her flower was stolen prepubescent
But she told herself she was okay with it
Because she thought that was the thing to do.
She had so much potential and she threw it all away.
But who am I to say this
We all destroy ourselves one way or another
It just looks different.

Broken Glass

I was a glass flower vase
And that little seed inside me was just starting to grow
I could feel it.
The dark damaged soil was finally creating something
     beautiful
It could've been a flower
Or fruit.
But then they dropped me
And I shattered
Into hundreds of pieces.
I tried to tape myself together
I tried super glue too
But you can't fix
     broken glass.

Tock Tick

The clock started melting
Time's flying by
    like the speed of
    light.
When did my limbs
    stretch so far?
When did I start
    hesitating before
    eating what I
    like?
When did my
    parents
    stop saying
    good-night?

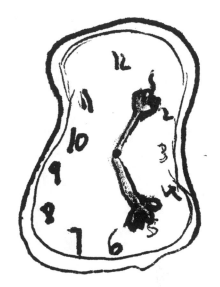

When did the innocents of the neighborhood stop meeting
    at that one rock
When did all those faces start to fade
When did our problems become real.
I broke my clock.
I don't want to see time pass like this.

9.8x2

This is why I don't do it
I don't open up
Because all it brings is pain
I try so hard to act like it's not real and that I feel nothing
But I can no longer pretend
It hurts all too much
There's a new heavy presence in my body and it feels like its
    dragging me down
Gravity must've gotten stronger

Playground

Skipping through my mind
Fond memories of fresh grass
Grazing toes
Giggles and puddles

Astronaut

We feel a deep craving to be something,
Someone.
We want to be remembered
Loved
And wanted.
When we were children, we thought it was possible
Easy
We could be anyone.
But as time grows
We start ~~accepting~~ that we aren't special
*thinking.
Our shadows will float over our heads
Our dream shadows of being perfect
Of being an astronaut
To save the world

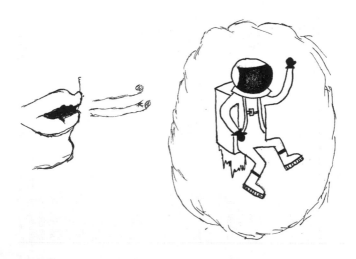

We watch these shadows with longing but then brush them
away before anyone sees because they are childish.
But some hold themselves to these standards
And break their minds trying to attain them.
While others float in the void of being no one and start
building a life in this vacuum- sealed bubble
I want to be someone
I want my parents to be proud
But it feels too late.

Piece 3

Passion and Heartache

Murder

She loved you.

That wasn't enough.

She changed for you.

You wanted more.

She killed someone to make you love her.

And now she's gone

She exists, soulless, wandering the earth as a corpse.
Purposeless.

You let her believe you were her purpose

They say time heals all, but time's passed, nothing healed,
she's still dead, she's still gone.

You twisted her arm, you helped her put the knife in her
heart

The blood is on your hands

You lit the match, you ignited her.

But you, you were the one who put it out.

It would appear she's back, alive, but our eyes deceive us
because now she's just a mere visitor in her own body,
she learned to continue to go on, but not to live.

There's no life left there.

Only flesh.

She killed herself to make you love her.

The Conniving Chef

You promised her the meal of her life.

She couldn't resist

She let you snatch her heart for the main course because you doused it in flavor, you warmed it up and made it feel alive.

You told her that her heart wasn't enough,

You "needed" more.

So she gave you her tears

You comforted her and said you needed the water to help you cook.

Who was she to question you? You were the chef.

But as time passed you weren't just warming her heart

You turned the stove up full blast.

You were burning it, letting it sizzle and tossing it in the air for mere fun

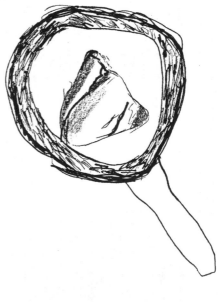

But she let you because you were the chef

Then you pulled out the knife

She watched as you butchered her heart

Then you threw it in the blender and left.
And now that's all she feels
Her heart in the blender.
You told her you were a chef
But now I see, you were a butcher man.

Omnipotent

My hearts beating so hard it could burn a hole through my
    chest
You have the power to do that
With a single word you can make me explode
And you don't even know it

Catch and Release Fisherman

Out on my common journey I depart filled with anxious
   excitement and hope
Grabbing my rod and bait, I set
   sail.
I imagine you swimming along
   happily with other fish
But that's not what I want
I want you in my hands, only mine.
I paddle out further, searching for
   you and dreaming what our
   time together will be like.
I spot you
My blood pumps with adrenaline
   as I cast out my bait.
Naively you latch on, I begin to reel
   you in
You resist a bit
That's my favorite part, when you
   play hard to get.
We do this for a while
But then you surrender
You're mine.
I finally have you, I'm overjoyed
But a few moments pass and I
   realize I don't really want you

It was the idea of you which I adored so much
When we are together the feeling fades.
Arrogantly I throw you back
I am a catch and release fisherman
I do it for the chase.
Don't be a fool
Don't believe the bait
Don't be the prey of the catch and release fisherman.
The chase is what I fish for, not love.

Disabled

Your love inflicted her with disability
She followed you blindly
She chased you recklessly
Your touch paralyzed her
Your love deafened the truth
She was no longer sane
Your love made her mad.

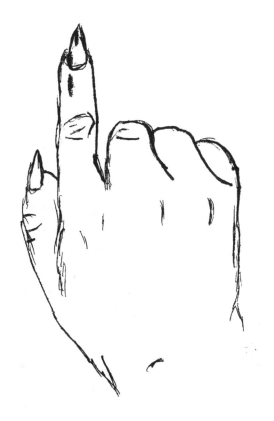

Lame

Why can't you just know how I feel?
I know I've lied to you which is on me
But I thought you would be able to see through me
Why do these things need to be verbally said when they can
be shown physically through actions
You must know
There's no way you can't
I know you aren't that oblivious

Compounds & Mixtures

We tend to mistake infatuation for love
Infatuation is when you are a good mixture
Individuals of a mixture can be physically separated
But love is when you are a compound
The elements in a compound can only be separated by
destroying the compound Physically, you cannot separate one

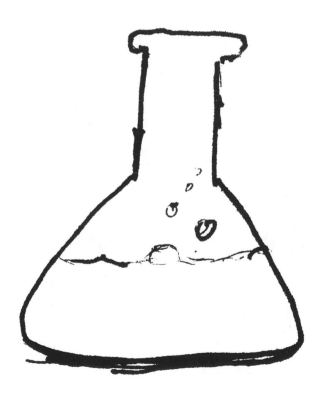

An Angel

She was as bright as the sun, her presence brought warmth, un-outshine-able by anyone else, but not competitively; it was natural she didn't control it, she emanated light more brightly than anyone I had ever met. She was the beginning, she was my first.

Infatuation

New beginnings are always filled with hope and excitement.

When you first meet a person who knows nothing about you, and you start talking, and it's like wow this new person is so interesting you crave to know more.

You get so invested in that person, you show them all your cool spots, tell them all your jokes and share all your interests.

But then slowly and all at once the spark's gone, there's no more to say, no more special places to share.

They start getting bored, I mean, after all, everyone desires excitement and pleasure. So they look for it and maybe find it in another person (which is cheating) but you can't blame them, they are just satisfying their hunger for excitement as a human being.

So now, once again, they are hooked to this new person who is oh so interesting, but there is only so much to a person, so they too will get boring.

It's a cycle that we naively repeat.

Bruno

I'm not ready to let you go
You became my normal
You were a part of my routine.

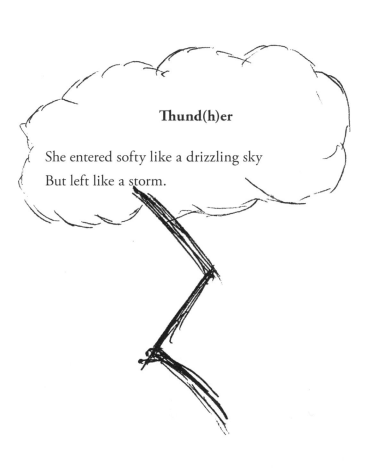

Thund(h)er

She entered softy like a drizzling sky
But left like a storm.

Moody

I think I love her

I don't believe in love

Why am I feeling this way?

I hate it

And the worst part is she doesn't even want me

Why throw my heart in the gutter when the gutter is already
full

God this hurts so much

But I can't let her see that either

They Would Survive

I thought we were supposed to love for the substance,
For the soul.
So why do we frown upon the pansexual and bi?
They love for the pages and text
Not for the covers
Or build
They have the most open of minds
The ability to love anyone
If the world were blind, they are the ones who would survive.

Morphine

Everything was black
Then I woke up.
Light shone through.
It felt like warm snowflakes were skipping through my veins
The pain was gone
I looked at my arm
There was an IV pumping morphine into my body.
I felt that same feeling again today
When you touched my hand and held it in your own
The pain was gone once again
You are my new morphine.
My feel-good.

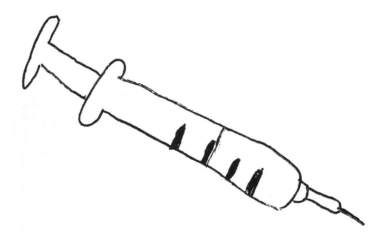

Blurred Focus

You hold my attention too strongly.
I'm not getting anything done.
When you're here you're all I see
All I hear
When you're gone you're all I can think about
I can't even call you a distraction
You've become my focus

House Flipper

I'll admit I wasn't too furnished
Or pretty
Or taken care of properly.
But it was me
I was an old home.
And you came in like you owned the place.
You wanted to make me "better"
And like a house flipper you broke down all my walls and
    bones.
You enjoyed it.
I felt every blow of your sledgehammer
Breaking me down slowly and all at once.

You did it
for your own
profit
With this you
ruined me
And I was
left there as
a completely
different
house
With no
bones
No love
No life.

Satanic

Devil on my shoulder
Devil on my tongue
You make me feel an awful way
But I am addicted to it.
Your tongue is venomous
And I'm your prey.
You inject me with poison
And to my knees I drop.
To hell and back we go
My body burns in flames.

Yum

Seeing you again was like a feast for the senses
But I must restrain myself from indulging
Because I cannot fall down that rabbit hole of your fake
reality again.
I myself need to become my own feast that I love.
My adoration of you feeds my hatred towards me.

Walking the Plank

I decided to finally open up
Just once
I did the thing
I jumped off the boat
I left ship for you
Knowingly jumping in the waters which brought me
discomfort
The water was cold
It made me feel weak
And the worst part is
You weren't even there to catch me
You were off about dancing and swimming amid these
waters
Waters which you were so comfortable in
There is no one to blame but me
I decided to jump
What did I think would happen?

.

We try too hard for the wrong people
We overthink their every punctuation
Their every movement
As if we're just a piece of meat we wish they wanted

Blah Blah Blah

I don't want your bullshit excuses
I don't want to hear it's not you it's me
Just tell me the truth and let me feel
So I can grieve and move on
I know you think it'll hurt me
You're not wrong
But I won't grow unless you tell me
Don't just leave me in the dark like a naive child

Weak Battery

I am tired
Our batteries have run out.
I should've known the energy loss would be inevitable
But still to the idea I clung
I thought a simple recharge could bring us back.
But we were too low
My negative overpowered your positive,
The balance was off.

Mind Reader

I want you to want me
But not because you know I want you to
But because you want to.
I want flowers
But I don't want to have to say I do
I want you to know.
But then again how can I expect such high standards?

Machu Picchu

Distance in a relationship does create mountains
But these mountains are not always treacherous.
They challenge us
They remind us the weight of our love
Of what life is like without that person
They can show us how high we'd climb for them
How many rivers we'd cross
And what we'd sacrifice.

Blanket

I get too wrapped up in it all
Whisper something nice
Show appreciation
And I'm yours

Gun Under the Table

The dinner was nice

You were lovely

But then I felt something graze my leg.

A handgun.

This dinner was amazing

You said all the right things and looked at me all the right
ways

But the whole time you had a gun under the table.

You had the power to blow it all up

And that's how it feels being with you

I love it.

But at any

moment

Any time

You have the

power to

ruin it all.

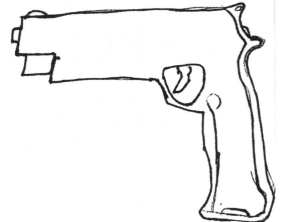

Rent

You're taking up too much space up there
You're making it chaotic
Stop running around
I wish you would just leave
But I now realize I am the one who must evict you.

Piece 4

Universal Affliction

A Smile like That

A smile like that.

It was a smile I had never seen before

A smile that made me sad (brought tears to my eyes), yet so happy at the same time.

It was the smiles of the children at a homeless shelter

The children who had so little but were smiling so much

They were the happiest, most cheerful children I had ever witnessed.

It brought me deep sorrow to think of these kids

I wish I could give them the world.

The thing that was so sad was that these kids were 10x happier with nothing than the kids I knew who had everything.

A simple haircut made them happy for days

While my neighbor cries because he didn't get the iPhone he wanted.

These children were eye-opening

They show you the real value of material.

We tend to get caught up in our suburban bubbles where our problems vary between Who has the newest clothes or better grades,

We need to get out of these bubbles

See the real world
We might think we are aware of the problems, but we truly
    are not until we go see them and spend time with them.
Then you will know
    A smile like one of those.

Super Women

The mothers looked tired

The bags under their eyes could hold an infant.

But when they saw their children, the tired look seemed to fade

They wore a smile that stretched across their entire face.

The bags remained, but in that moment, they weren't as apparent.

Their lives were tough

But they were tougher

They would do anything for their kids

They were the real, live super women

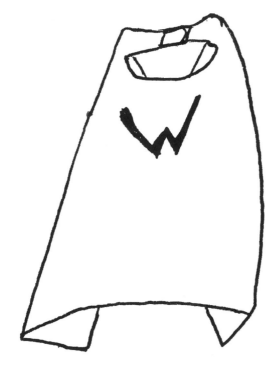

Standards

She's a whore!

We want more

Pull your skirt down!

Don't frown

Wear more makeup!

You look like a clown

Hide that stretch mark!

You're too dark

Have a child!

Don't be wild

Sleep with me!

You should always agree

You slept with him?!

You're too grim

He slept with her?

He's a man for sure

You won't have sex with me?

You're a bore

Please walk out the door.

Usual

I am not okay

"Girls say that every day".

I am not okay

"It's because your mind's astray".

I am not okay

"Maybe you should obey".

I am not okay

"Sleep with me anyway".

Roaring Twenties

We're all stuck living in the Gatsby novel
Chasing the same thing
The American dream.
While drowning ourselves with antidepressants and alcohol
Reaching for our own green lights
And waiting for the ring of a phone call.
Our minds set high but our bodies getting no where
Showing off so no one notices how hollow we really are
And using anything and everything for our own gain.
And one day while swimming amidst our own pools of
    "wealth"
We, too, will be killed by our own mistakes.

Adopt

They left him on the shelf too long
Dust started settling
They thought he'd lost his value
He did too
I found him in the trash
Junk all over him
I couldn't leave him there
I took him home
All it took was a wash and a little shining up
He was still a trophy
He was still gold
All it takes is a little noticing

Silly Me

I am currently in Paris

Sitting in front of the Eiffel Tower

But that's not what draws my attention

It's the people taking photos.

I don't think they've even seen the Eiffel Tower

Or that they ever will

Just the photos on their phones with their faces as the main
focus.

What's the point of traveling here to not even look at
something so beautiful?

Oh wait

My bad

The likes

The comments

That's the value these
days.

Silly me.

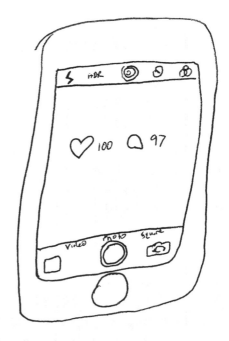

What a Year

2018 wasn't a good year

It was a year shootings became casual

It was a year children dying became a common reoccurrence

It was a year when we heard about massacres, it was like hearing a baby was born

It was a year when hearing about tear gas being deployed into crowds of people, we barely batted an eye.

I guess every year has its issues

I just really saw the problems more this year

I guess it's going to keep getting worse.

Can't wait for 2019.

Run

Without batting an eye, they rush over me
Like hungry New Yorkers

It's June 5th 2019

40 Sudanese bodies were just thrown into a river

Over 200 people just died

Uncountable women were just raped

They were fighting

They were protesting

They were peaceful

Their names should live on

But how is it possible to remember so many names?

How is anyone going to memorize that many faces?

People die every fucking day and we barely know a soul.

Is this what life is supposed to be like?

You die living a life of nothing,

No one remembers your name.

You die fighting for your country,

No one remembers your name.

So what the hell is the point of doing anything if no one is
    going to remember you?

But I forgot to mention the fact that Sudan has now been
    removed from the UN

The government that did this will be terminated.

Those people that died are creating better lives for the next.

Not everyone died; their families are still alive and will
    remember them

Anyone who knew them will mourn.

They might've died not knowing it

But they sure did it.

Piece 5

Everything (and Nothing) Else

Secrets

We tell strangers our secrets because we hope they'll disappear with them.

Writing

I write when I am filled with emotion

When I am sad

When I am angry

I write because I am not good at talking about my feelings.

I don't like seeming weak in the eyes of others

And if I talk, I might cry

And if I cry, I might create an ocean

So I will continue to waste ink

And move this pen along this paper till I am numb

And there are no more tears left to cry.

Silence

Silence is an odd thing

It can make us feel awkward in a group

But it can also make us feel wanted.

The idea that someone only wants you for your presence

rather than their entertainment

A comfortable silence is a hard one to attain

But to be able to share it is truly a gift.

Out of Body Out of Mind

When I write it's like I'm not in my body
I'm a quiet lurker.
I watch my body and see all the mistakes she makes
And how arrogant and selfish she is
She's just another extremely flawed character that I write
about
When my pencil's on the paper I can see deeper
And feel deeper.
But then I lift up the pencil
And am forced back into my body
And then I just repeat the same mistakes.
I wish I could be out of my body more
I wish I could write forever.

I Envy Those Eyes

Her eyes were hard to follow
They would be looking into your eyes
But not directly.
She would look at your body
But not the outside
She was looking through us
She didn't see an exterior.
She saw people for their true intentions
Their raw flesh and their raw passion.
Her eyes were like hands
They had the power to rip you apart
But instead they held you gently.

Losing Someone

There're 3 kinds of people when it comes to grieving the loss of someone.

For some it fades quickly, like a chapter of a book, they lightly grieve then turn the page.

For others it stays within them permanently like a tattoo, but a deep one that is infected and brings a deep scorching pain that is constant and lasts forever.

And for the resilient ones, they try to put it away into a shoe box deep in their closet thinking the box won't break,
For months, it seems as if they are okay and strong but then one day when they finally realize that the person is really gone, that box will break, as will they, and the pain and emotion will be intolerable and they will finally grieve.

But in reality, there aren't 3 ways of grieving, there're 3 kinds of people that bring out each type of grieving:

The people you touch
The people you feel
The people who live in you

Old Angel

I remember her crinkled eyes
Full of curiosity
They were blue from age
I think that's why I wish I had blue eyes.
I remember her voice
Like a melody to my ears
Her voice spilt knowledge.
I remember her ears
Oh her ears
They would listen to me for hours.

I remember her heavy arms
That were once so slim and beautiful
They would hold me so close.
I remember her stomach
The way it would jiggle when she laughed
It never really stopped jiggling.
Don't even get me started on her laugh
It was the most wholesome noise I had ever heard
I could listen to it endlessly.
I think of her a lot
Almost too much
I think it's because the idea of forgetting her seems too scary
I don't want to move on.

Barbie World

It's a toy town, we're all Barbies,

We go home to our play houses with our plastic families

Your parents look so in love!

Smile!

Don't stay out too long you might melt!

You need to look pretty

Your head's on backwards but no one notices the difference

The kids are coming to play

Your life is perfect

We all are

We have to be

But we all know what happens when the lights turn off

The paint comes off

The smiles fade

The perfect parents drown their "love" with liquor and affairs

Bills appear from the hidden drawers
Your Kens are in another room with another doll
The eye makeup smears with tears
But hurry wipe it away, the sun's coming up!

Small Towns

I don't like where I live
It's a small bubble
Everyone knows you by name
And it'll come out of their mouths at least once a day

Euphoric

Light headed
Heavy footed
We walk along the water
Feeling nothing but the ground beneath our feet and the
humid air breathing on our skin
The fire in our hands burning so great
I want to stay here forever.

The end. That was my mind, my thoughts, my everything. This is me as an open book. I hope you relate and maybe don't feel as alone. Thank you for reading :).